By Carroll Lane Fenton and Mildred Adams Fenton

GIANTS OF GEOLOGY

THE LAND WE LIVE ON

OUR CHANGING WEATHER

PREHISTORIC ZOO

THE ROCK BOOK

ROCKS AND THEIR STORIES

THE FOSSIL BOOK

By Carroll Lane Fenton

OUR AMAZING EARTH

OUR LIVING WORLD

PREHISTORIC ZOO

Dinosaurs were the strangest creatures in the prehistoric zoo. This dinosaur had a bony crest on its head. (**3**)

4

PREHISTORIC
ZOO

By

CARROLL LANE FENTON

and

MILDRED ADAMS FENTON

Doubleday & Company, Inc.
Garden City, New York

CONTENTS

WELCOME TO
THE PREHISTORIC ZOO

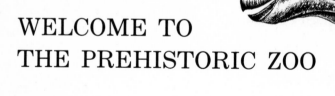

When we visit a zoo or go to the circus
we see animals that come
from many, many parts of the world.
Another kind of zoo may be seen
in museums of natural history.
This zoo contains animals
which we sometimes call "prehistoric,"
and sometimes call "fossil."
"Prehistoric" tells us that the creatures lived
long before human beings learned
to write or to make books.
"Fossil" means that the ancient animals
left teeth, bones, and even footprints
in beds of mud, sand, or soil
that have turned into rock.

10

This book will take you through a zoo
where you will find prehistoric animals
near their modern relatives.
You also will see beasts, birds, and reptiles
that were different from anything
that is alive today.
You might never suspect
that such creatures existed
if you could not find them
in our prehistoric zoo.

This strange beast from South America has no living relatives.
6–F)

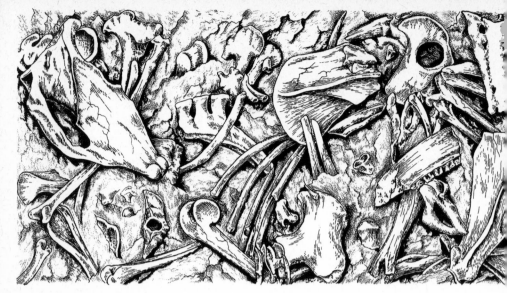

Fossil bones in a slab of rock from Nebraska. (**5–D**)

ANIMALS FOR ANCIENT ZOOS

Strange animals in modern zoos
are caught by hunters.
But creatures in prehistoric zoos
must be dug out of the ground.
Men dig up bones, skulls, teeth,
and even footprints
and send them to museums.
There scientists study the ancient fossils
and compare them with living animals.
Then the skulls, teeth, and bones
are fitted together.

12

Finally, the scientists draw pictures
to show what the ancient creatures
looked like when they were alive.
Such pictures are called restorations.
On page 12 are some fossil bones and a skull
just as they came from the ground.
Here is a restoration (RES to RAY shun).
It turns the fossil bones into a rhinoceros
for our prehistoric zoo.
Herds of small rhinoceroses like this one
lived in the region we call Nebraska
ages and ages ago.

This rhinoceros is restored from the bones shown on page 12. **(5–D)**

WHEN DID THEY LIVE?

Some prehistoric animals were common
a few thousand years ago,
but others are many, many times older.
To discover when different animals lived
notice the number, or the number and letter,
after the explanation of each picture.
Then turn to page 125
and find the same number or letter
in the Calendar of Ancient Ages.
For example, the rhinoceros on page 13
has the number and letter (5–D).
When you turn to page 125, you find
that (5) is the Tertiary period, or age.
(D) is the Miocene epoch, which began
about 28 million years ago
and lasted for 16 million years.
Thus the number and letter (5–D) tell us
that the rhinoceros lived in Miocene times,
less than 28 million years ago.

14

A modern elephant from Asia. (**6–G**)

THE ELEPHANT FAMILY

Elephants are the largest creatures
to be seen in circuses or zoos.
Modern elephants have big ears
and long trunks instead of noses.
Full-grown elephants also are tall,
with thick legs to hold their heavy bodies,
which weigh several tons.
The front teeth have become tusks.
Some tusks are short, but others are long
and weigh more than 200 pounds.

Although most modern elephants are big,
the elephant family began
with small, piglike animals
that had no trunks or tusks
and were only 2 feet tall at the shoulder.
These piglike creatures lived in Egypt.
As years went by, they had young ones
that were larger and had longer snouts.
The front teeth grew longer, too,
until they became small tusks
on both the upper and lower jaws.
At last some of the animals
began to resemble small elephants.
Those called Palaeomastodon (PAY lee o MAS toe d
were about 3 feet tall at the shoulder.
The animals probably lived on swampy land
and ate soft, juicy plants
that grew near the water.

The elephant family began with this animal, which was about 2 feet high. It lived in ancient Egypt. (**5–B, C**)

The second stage in the development of elephants. This creature, Palaeomastodon, had a short trunk and short tusks, and was about 3 feet tall. (**5–C**)

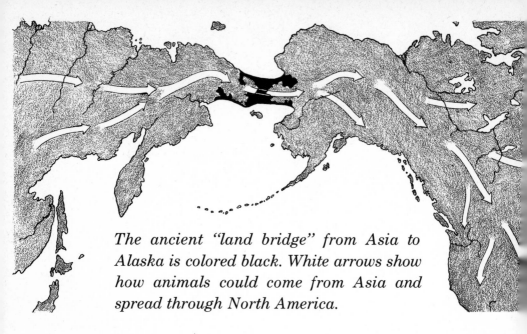

The ancient "land bridge" from Asia to Alaska is colored black. White arrows show how animals could come from Asia and spread through North America.

AN AMERICAN TUSKER

The elephant family kept on changing
for millions and millions of years.
Bodies grew bigger and bigger.
Trunks became longer and longer,
and the upper tusks became large.
The changing animals also wandered
away from their homes in Egypt.
Some kinds went to Europe.
Other kinds wandered across Asia.
At last they crossed a strip of land
that ran from Asia to North America
during some prehistoric ages.

The map on page 18 shows this "land bridge."
Here is one of the first members of the
elephant family that crossed this bridge
and lived in North America.
This animal was 6 or 7 feet tall.
It had two tusks on its upper jaws.
It had two more tusks on its lower jaws,
which were very long.
We think the lower tusks were diggers.
They dug up roots and juicy swamp plants
which this creature liked to eat.

*This was one of the first members of the elephant family in
America.* (**5–E**)

COLUMBIAN MAMMOTH

Mammoths were real elephants,
with long trunks and big tusks
on their upper jaws.
Mammoths developed millions of years
after the long-jawed beast with four tusks
came to North America.
Some mammoths were not very large.
Others became more than 13 feet tall,
which means that they were much bigger
than elephants that live today.
Columbian mammoths came in between,
for only a few became much more
than 10 feet high at the shoulder.
Columbian mammoths once were common
in the southwestern United States and Mexico.
The largest kinds of mammoths ranged northward
to Nebraska and Colorado.
Ancient hunters sometimes killed these beasts
with stone axes and spears.

The Columbian mammoth was an elephant that sometimes grew more than 10 feet high. This one is shown in southern California, in country that is now desert. **(6–F)**

WOOLLY MAMMOTH

Columbian mammoths lived in places
where winters did not become very cold.
Woolly mammoths were northern animals.
They ranged across Europe and northern Asia,
and from Alaska to Indiana.
Winters grew cold in most of these regions,
and the ground was covered with snow.
Woolly mammoths did not mind the cold weather.
They had undercoats of thick, warm wool.
They had outer coats of coarse brown hair
that kept snow and rain out of their wool.
The animals carried their big heads high,
but their backs sloped down to their tails.
Woolly mammoths sometimes fell into cracks
and were preserved in frozen ground.

These big, frozen fossils
still have their flesh, skin, and hair.
They show us just what the animals looked like
when they were alive.

The woolly mammoth had a coat of coarse hair over its wool. The animal lived in cold countries during the Ice Age. (**6–F**)

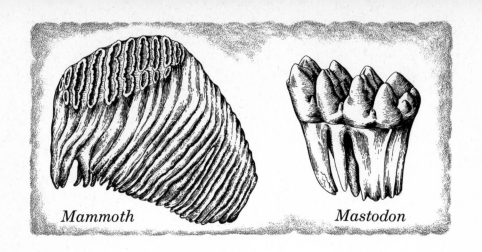

A mammoth's tooth is different from the tooth of a mastodon. **(6–F)**

AMERICAN MASTODON

Mastodons looked like shaggy mammoths
that were 7, 8, or 9 feet tall.
But mastodons had low foreheads
and their tusks were not very long.
Their teeth also were different
from the grinding teeth of mammoths.
Mammoths had big, flat teeth
with almost no roots,
but with ridges across the top.
The teeth of mastodons were smaller.
They had long roots and irregular tops
covered with cone-shaped bumps.

24

Mastodons that lived in Africa, Europe,
and Asia died out in Pliocene (PLY o seen) times.
American mastodons were more hardy,
for they kept on living until
a few thousand years ago.
The animals roamed through forests.
They crossed prairies and mountain ranges.
They waded into swamps to eat plants.
Sometimes mastodons sank into the mud
and could not get out again.
When the animals died, their flesh decayed
but their bones and teeth became fossils.

The American mastodon often lived in woodlands. (**6–F**)

The armadillo's skin has become shields and rings of armor. (**6–G**

ARMADILLOS

Most armadillos live in South America,
but one kind comes as far northward
as Texas and Louisiana.
Armadillo is a Spanish word
that means "small animal in armor."
Common armadillos deserve this name.
They are short-legged animals, a little more
than 2 feet long from their noses
to the tips of their tails.
Their skin has become curved shields
and jointed rings of bony armor.

26

When something alarms an armadillo,
it rolls itself into a ball.
This makes the armor cover its body
so the creature cannot be harmed.
Ancient armadillos had armored skin, too.
Some kinds also developed horns on their heads,
but others became larger and larger.
The largest living armadillo
is 4 feet 6 inches long
and weighs about 100 pounds.
But one ancient kind of armadillo
was as large as a rhinoceros
and weighed at least 4,000 pounds.
This giant lived in South America
at about the time Columbian mammoths
first came to the United States.

*This ancient armadillo
had four horns
on its head.* (**6–F**)

GLYPTODONTS

These queer beasts looked like armadillos
and were related to them.
But every glyptodont (GLIP toe dahnt)
had a deep, blunt head,
and the armor that covered its body
had become one big, hard shell.
Some glyptodonts were 6 to 9 feet long
and had thick, short tails.
Other kinds had longer tails
that ended in bony spikes.
When an enemy attacked a glyptodont,
the animal swung its tail like a war club.
One blow from that sharp-spiked club
was enough to kill any creature
that dared to attack a glyptodont.

28

yptodonts were big animals related to armadillos. Some glypto-nts became 9 feet long. Others were 12 to 15 feet long and had ils that ended in spikes. Most of these animals lived in South nerica. (**6–F**)

The tree sloth hangs from branches and moves very slowly. (**6–G**)

TREE SLOTHS

If someone says you "move like a sloth,"
he means that you move very slowly.
Sloths are short-tailed animals
that are related to armadillos.
They live in the big, thick forests
of South and Central America.
There the sloths hang upside down
and feed on leaves of trees.
The animals can climb slowly,
but they often hang from one branch
for hours or even days at a time.
They seem too lazy or too stupid
to climb about or nibble leaves.

30

A small ground sloth, about 3 feet 3 inches tall. (**6–F**)

GROUND SLOTHS

Sloths of modern times hang in trees,
but the sloths in our prehistoric zoo
always lived on the ground.
The kind you see here slept in caves.
In the daytime it went out to eat plants
that grew on dry hillsides.
This ground sloth was 3 feet 6 inches tall
when it stood on all four feet.
It had brownish hair, long forelegs,
and very large hind feet.

The giant ground sloth was 18 to 20 feet long. **(6–F)**

GIANT GROUND SLOTH

Cave ground sloths were not very large,
but some of their relatives
became huge animals
with thick, barrel-shaped bodies.
The giant was Megatherium (MEG a THEE ri um),
whose scientific name means "big beast."
Megatherium grew to be 20 feet long
and weighed at least 10,000 pounds.
He walked on the sides and backs of his feet,
which had enormous claws.
Megatherium sat up to pull leaves from trees
or to strike enemies with his forefeet.
But he crouched down when he wanted
to walk or to eat plants
that grew on the ground.

The bison, or buffalo, once was common in the West. (**6–G**)

BISON, OR BUFFALO

The proper name for these animals is bison,
but we usually call them buffaloes.
Buffaloes are big, cowlike animals.
They used to live in huge herds
that roamed across the western plains.
Indians killed buffaloes for meat.
Tents, or tipis, were made from the skins,
which also were used for robes
and many other things.
Indian children often caught buffalo calves
and kept them as pets.

34

Nowadays, many calves are born in zoos,
where boys and girls may watch them.
Buffalo calves have light brown hair,
but full-grown animals are dark brown.
The hair on their hind quarters is short,
but the hair is long and woolly
on their forelegs, shoulders, and heads.

This bison calf, about one week old, was born in a zoo. (**6–G**)

A straight-horned bison and a stone spear point. Ancient men used spears like this when they hunted the bison. (**6–F**)

TWO ANCIENT BISON

Many different kinds of bison
lived during the prehistoric time, or epoch,
which we often call the Ice Age.
Some of these ancient bison
resembled our modern buffalo.
Other kinds had higher humps,
or horns that spread sideways
instead of curving upward.

36

Straight-horned bison were often killed
by people who lived in the West
long before the Indians came.
The giant bison was 7 feet tall at its hump.
This means that the animal
was 12 to 18 inches taller
than the modern bison on page 34.
The giant bison's horns were 6 feet wide.
Herds of these big animals ranged
from Oregon to Texas and Florida
less than 50 thousand years ago.

A giant bison with horns 6 to 7 feet wide. (**6–F**)

GIRAFFE AND OKAPI

Many zoos have spotted giraffes,
with long, slender necks and legs.
Some zoos also have okapis.
The okapi (o KAH pi) is related to giraffes,
but its neck and legs are not so long
and it is not spotted.
Both okapis and giraffes have horns
made of bone covered with skin.
Okapis live in thick, shady forests
of central Africa.
Giraffes like grassy country, or veld (velt),
which is like our plains and prairies.
There the giraffes roam in herds
and feed upon leaves or twigs
that grow near the tops of trees.

Giraffe

Okapi

A modern giraffe and an okapi. (**6–G**)

ANCIENT OKAPIS

Prehistoric relatives of giraffes
lived in Africa, Asia, and Europe.
Some kinds were tall and had long necks.
Others looked like okapis
with slender, sharp-pointed horns.
Here is a prehistoric okapi
that lived in southern Europe and Asia
millions of years ago.
Nearby is an okapi-like creature
called Sivatherium (see vah THEE ri um).
It resembled a long-legged ox
with an okapi's pointed head
and four skin-covered horns.
Two of the horns were pointed,
but the others were long and wide.
Sivatherium lived in southern Asia
when mammoths and mastodons were common
in North America.

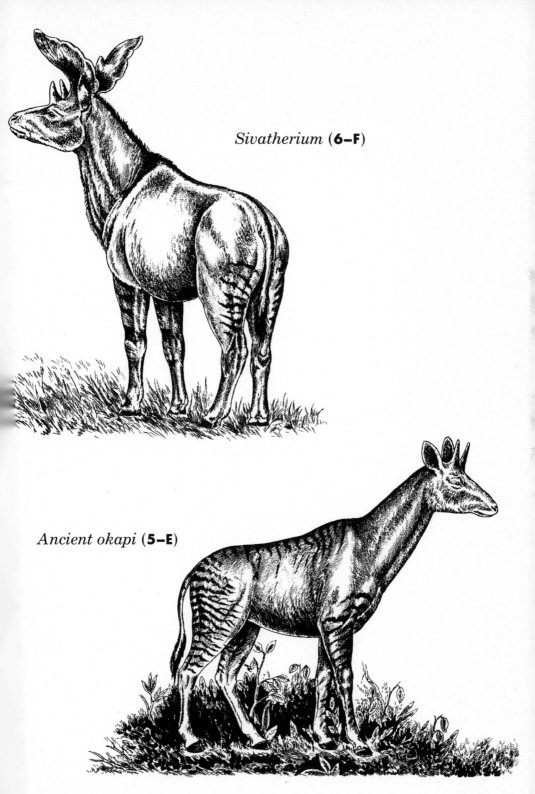

Sivatherium (**6–F**)

Ancient okapi (**5–E**)

Two prehistoric relatives of giraffes.

The American elk is a big deer. (**6–G**)

AMERICAN AND IRISH ELK

The American elk is a big brown deer
that lives among western mountains.
It becomes 5 feet tall at its shoulders
and has long, branched antlers.
The Irish elk was a still bigger deer.
It lived in Europe during the Ice Age
and for many years afterward,
but it never came to North America.

Irish elk were 12 to 18 inches taller
than the largest American elk.
The Irish elk also had huge antlers
that spread out and then branched,
and were 7 to 8 feet wide.
No other deer ever had antlers
as big as those of the Irish elk.

The ancient Irish elk had antlers 7 to 8 feet wide. (**6–F, G**)

MODERN CAMELS

Camels are long-legged beasts
that have thick, soft pads on their feet
and one or two humps on their backs.
Pads help the animals walk on deserts
without slipping in loose sand.
Camels' humps are like spongy bags
that can be filled with fat.
When the animals have plenty to eat
they turn some of their food into fat
and store it in their humps.
Then, when food becomes scarce,
this stored-up fat is used.
Camels can also drink a great deal
and store water which they don't need
in the lining of their stomachs.
The animals use this stored-up water
when they cross broad deserts
where there is almost nothing to drink.

Modern camels with two humps are found in central Asia, but one-humped camels live in western Asia and Africa. The humps are used to store up fat when the animals have plenty to eat. (**6–G**)

These small camels from ancient Nebraska looked like antelopes about 2 feet tall. (**5–D**)

HOW CAMELS BEGAN

Camels now live in Africa and Asia,
but the camel family began
in North America.
The first members of the family
were little animals that looked
like baby goats, or short-tailed lambs
with coats of hair instead of wool.
Later came slender animals
that resembled hornless antelopes
about 2 feet tall at their shoulders.

46

Some of these early camels had long necks,
but their hoofs were sharp.
They had no foot-pads
to help them walk across sand,
and no humps for storing fat.
Big herds of these small humpless camels
roamed through the West millions of years
before mammoths, ground sloths, and bison
began to live there.
Humpless camels also went to South America.
Some of their descendants,
called the guanaco (gwa NAH ko) and llama,
are still common in South America.

o humpless camels from the Badlands of South Dakota. (**5–C**)

GIRAFFE CAMELS

Real giraffes and okapis never lived
in North or South America.
But some ancient camels developed
such long legs and such very long necks
that we call them giraffe camels.
The first giraffe camels were only 5 feet tall
but they had young ones that grew taller.
This happened over and over again
during thousands and millions of years.
At last some giraffe camels became so tall
that they could nibble leaves and twigs
that grew more than 12 feet above the ground.
Herds of these tall, long-necked camels
lived in the regions which we now
know as Nebraska and Colorado.

This ancient giraffe camel could eat leaves from branches 12 feet above the ground. (**5–D**)

*A giant pig
and its skull.* (**5–C**)

GIANT PIGS

The wild pigs which we see in zoos
come from Africa and Asia.
But the animals called giant pigs
lived in Europe and North America, too.
The first giant pigs were not real giants,
for they were smaller than many hogs
that are now kept on farms.
Other giant pigs were huge, ugly beasts
with long heads and thick tusks,
and bony lumps on their cheeks and jaws.

50

The largest giant pigs were 7 feet tall
and weighed more than a ton.
These animals also lived in Nebraska.
There they roamed about, eating plants
or digging roots out of the ground.
Can you imagine a herd of giant pigs?
Do you suppose they pushed each other about?
Do you think they grunted and quarreled
when several animals
wanted to eat the same root?

The largest giant pig was 7 feet tall. (**5–D**)

EVEN-TOED AND ODD-TOED

Let's look once more at the animals
shown on pages 34 to 51.
All these creatures have hoofs on their feet,
not sharp claws or nails.
Some animals have two hoofs and two toes.
Other animals, such as bison, have four toes,
though only two are large.
Two and four are "even" numbers,
so we put creatures with two or four toes
together as even-toed animals with hoofs.
One, three, and five are "odd" numbers.
Creatures with one, three, or five hoofs
on two feet or on all four feet
belong to the odd-toed animals.
Horses are odd-toed animals,
for they have only one toe on each foot.
Cattle and pigs have four toes.
This tells us that they belong with bison,
among even-toed animals that have hoofs.

52

The horse is an odd-toed animal, with one toe and hoof on each foot. Cattle are even-toed, for they have two large toes and two small ones on each foot. (**6–G**)

The modern rhinoceros is an odd-toed animal with one or two horns on its nose. (**6–G**)

WOOLLY RHINOCEROS

The rhinoceros is an odd-toed animal
with three toes and hoofs on each foot.
He has one or two horns on his nose,
and his skin is so thick and stiff
that it resembles an armadillo's armor.
Modern rhinoceroses live in warm countries,
but some of their ancient relatives
were not so particular.

54

The woolly rhinoceros, for example,
roamed across northern Asia and Europe
during the Ice Age, or Ice Epoch,
when climates often became very cold.
Woolly mammoths also lived in the Ice Age.
Both mammoths and rhinoceroses
had thick coats of wool that kept them warm
during the coldest weather.
The animals hid in forests during storms,
but they walked about looking for food
while the ground was covered with snow.

The woolly rhinoceros lived in Europe and Asia during the Ice Age. (**6–F**)

THE BIGGEST RHINOCEROS

An Indian rhinoceros of modern times
may be 5 feet tall at its shoulders
and may weigh more than 4,000 pounds.
Most prehistoric rhinoceroses
were no larger than the Indian species,
and many were a good deal smaller.
But a rhinoceros that once lived in Asia
was bigger than any mammoth.
This animal, which had no horns,
is called a baluchithere (ba LOO chi THEER).
It stood 18 feet high at the shoulder.
Its head was almost 5 feet long,
and its thigh bone was taller than most men.
When the baluchithere stretched its neck
it could eat leaves and twigs from trees
at least 25 feet above the ground.

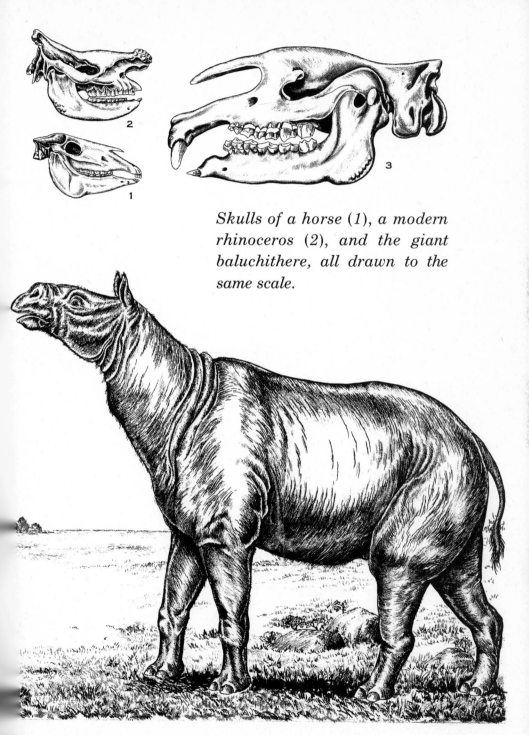

Skulls of a horse (1), a modern rhinoceros (2), and the giant baluchithere, all drawn to the same scale.

...he giant rhinoceros, or baluchithere, was 18 feet tall at the ...oulder, and its head was almost 5 feet long. There was no horn ... the nose. (**5–C**)

SIX BONY HORNS

Long before baluchitheres lived in Asia
this queer animal munched plants
in the western United States.
We call him Six-horns because
he has no common name
and no living relatives.
He was shaped like a rhinoceros,
but he had five toes on every foot, not three.
His head was very long and low,
and his little brain was very stupid.
He fought other beasts with his six bony horns
that were covered with skin.
He also slashed at his enemies
with dagger-shaped teeth
that grew from his upper jaw.
Such teeth were good for fighting,
but not for munching food.

ix-horns was a stupid animal about as large as a rhinoceros.
'is blunt horns were made of bone covered with skin. (**5–B**)

A scene in the Badlands of South Dakota.

BEASTS OF THE BADLANDS

When you cross the state of South Dakota,
you may spend a day or two in the Badlands.
Badlands are bare, beautiful places
where rain has worn beds of clay
into ridges, peaks, and narrow valleys
that are often called box canyons.
In ancient times, the Badlands were prairies
where rivers often overflowed
and covered the ground with mud.
Herds of animals also roamed on the prairies.
When these ancient animals died,
the mud often covered their bodies.

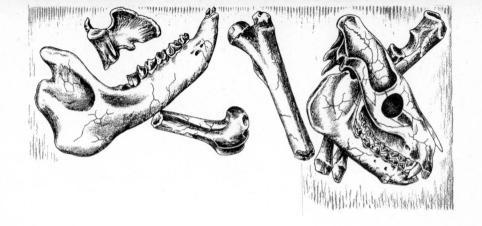

Then their bones and teeth became fossils,
which petrified, or "turned into stone."
Here are some petrified fossils
that were found in the Badlands.
One fossil is a rhinoceros jaw.
The other fossils belong to an even-toed animal
known as an oreodon (o REE o don).
Huge herds of small oreodons
ate plants on ancient prairies
that have become the Badlands.

An oreodon from the Badlands was 16 inches tall. (**5–C**)

GIANT BEASTS, OR TITANOTHERES

Oreodons were the commonest animals
found in the Badlands,
but titanotheres were the largest.
The word titanothere (TY tan o THEER)
means "giant beast," and
these animals deserved their name.
They looked like huge rhinoceroses
that were 7 to 8 feet tall,
and weighed more than many elephants.
Titanotheres lived in herds
and ate leaves of trees and tall bushes.
On hot days, the animals lay in the shade.
When they became angry, they fought
with pairs of skin-covered horns
that grew on their noses.

The horns were broad and blunt, not sharp,
but they could give harder blows
than the horns of any rhinoceros.

ese titanotheres resembled rhinoceroses but weighed more than
any circus elephants. (**5–C**)

A HOOFED ANIMAL
WITH CLAWS

Most animals with claws catch prey and eat it
or dig holes in the ground.
But this beast, called Moropus (mo RO pus),
ate leaves of bushes or low trees
and was much too large to burrow.
Moropus lived on ancient prairies.
His bones and teeth show that he belonged
among hoofed animals that ate plants
and had an odd number of toes.
No one knows why the hoofs of Moropus
had turned into claws
or just what he did with them.
Perhaps Moropus used them to dig roots.

Perhaps he used his claws to fight enemies
that sneaked up and tried to kill him
while he was nibbling leaves.

*Moropus was a plant-eater with claws instead of hoofs. This
animal lived at the same time as the rhinoceros on page 13.* (**5–D**)

Zebras are striped horses that now live in Africa. (**6–G**)

WILD HORSES

Wild horses of two different types
are seen in many zoos.
The type we know best consists of zebras,
which come from Africa.
There are several kinds of zebras.
All are pretty, striped animals
more than 4 feet tall at their shoulders.

66

Their short manes stand up stiffly
and the hair on their tails is not long.
Siberian wild horses come from the plains
of Siberia, in northern Asia.
These animals also have short manes,
but their coats are reddish or yellowish brown
and their lower legs are dark.
Siberian horses are not as tall as zebras,
but their bodies and heads are larger,
and their winter hair is long and furry.
Wild horses need warm winter coats,
for the weather often becomes very cold
on the plains of Siberia.

The Siberian wild horse comes from Asia. **(6–G)**

THE HORSE FAMILY AND HOW IT BEGAN

Horses are large, long-legged animals
that have only one toe on each foot
and one big, rounded hoof.
Ponies are one-toed animals, too.
So are donkeys, or burros, and wild asses,
which say "hee-haw" and have long ears.
All these animals resemble horses.
All have similar skulls and teeth,
and similar bones in their legs.
These resemblances explain why we say
that horses, ponies, donkeys, and wild asses
are related to each other
and belong to the horse family.

68

The horse family began with animals
which we often call eohippus (EE o hip us).
This name means "dawn horse" or "first horse."
Some dawn horses were as big as collie dogs,
but others were smaller than foxes.
All dawn horses had four toes on each forefoot
but only three toes behind.
This shows that they were odd-toed animals.
Herds of dawn horses lived in Europe,
as well as in Colorado, Wyoming,
and other parts of the West.

The dawn horse, or eohippus, had four toes on each front foot but three behind. (**5–B**)

THREE-TOED HORSES

Dawn horses lived for millions of years,
and they had many colts, or young ones.
Some colts were like their parents.
Others were taller or grew bigger bodies,
or had larger middle toes.
These changes went on year after year,
until some colts became different animals,
which we call Mesohippus (MES o HIP us).
Mesohippus means "middle horse,"
but this does not tell much
about these animals.
Mesohippus was a small, graceful creature
about 2 feet tall at its shoulders.
Its slender head was horselike.
Its feet had only three toes,
and each middle toe was larger
than the toes beside it.
Mesohippus used all three toes,
especially when he walked on soft ground.

Small three-toed horses, found in the Badlands of South Dakota.
(5–C)

FROM THREE TOES TO ONE

Mesohippus lived when titanotheres
roamed on prairies that now are the Badlands.
But as ages went by, horses kept on changing.
They developed larger and larger bodies,
and longer and longer heads.
Their middle toes became so long
that the side toes did not touch the ground.
At last the side toes disappeared,
and the animals became real horses.
The picture on page 73 shows
the dawn horse and Mesohippus.
It also shows a larger three-toed horse
and the first horse that had
only one toe on each foot.
All these animals lived in North America.
The first one-toed horses roamed the West
during the Pliocene (PLY o seen) epoch,
about 10 million years ago.

One of the first one-toed horses (**5–E**)

Large three-toed horse (**5–D**)

Small three-toed horse (**5–C**)

Dawn horse (**5–B**)

The bobcat is a modern carnivore. (**6–G**)

MEAT-EATERS, OR CARNIVORES

Zebras eat grass, giraffes nibble leaves,
and camels like almost anything
from dried fruit and hay to thorny twigs.
But many animals in zoos feed on meat.
Such creatures are called carnivores,
a name that means "meat-eaters."
Tigers, lions, and house cats are carnivores.
So are leopards, wolves, and bears.
You can tell most carnivores by their teeth,
which are sharp and are used to bite meat.
Many carnivores also have curved claws
which they use to catch their prey.

74

Cats show their claws when they play,
and their teeth may be seen when they yawn.
A dog shows his teeth when he feels hot
and opens his mouth to pant.
You can see the teeth of ancient carnivores
by looking at their skulls in museums.
The teeth also show in pictures
like those on pages 83 and 85.

*he wolf is a doglike carnivore with teeth for biting and cutting
*eat. This is a timber wolf. Small wolves called coyotes are com-
on on prairies and grassy plains. (**6–G**)

*Ectoconus, heigh
17 inches.*

*This awkward animal was neither a carnivore nor a hoofed
plant-eater.* (**5–A**)

WHAT DID THEY EAT?

When you look at these animals
can you tell what they ate?
If you can't tell, you have made a discovery.
You have discovered that some early beasts
had not become real plant-eaters
or real carnivores.
Instead, these beasts had teeth
that could chew fruit, leaves, juicy stems,
or the meat of other animals
that were small and easy to catch.

76

The toes of these beasts also were covered
with things that were not quite claws
and certainly were not hoofs.
Some of these in-between beasts
were no bigger than cats or dogs.
Others became quite large.
The clumsy animal called Barylambda (ba ry LAM da)
was about 8 feet long.

primitive animal about 8 feet long. Its name is Barylambda.
–A)

CREODONTS

The first real carnivores
had both claws and teeth for cutting meat.
But the animals were not big, like lions,
or swift and clever, like wolves.
We call these beasts creodonts (KREE o donts),
for they have no everyday name.
Here are three creodonts that lived in the West
in the days when dawn horses were common.
Don't you think these ancient carnivores
look clumsy as well as stupid?
Are you surprised when we tell you
that creodonts were not closely related
to lions, tigers, wolves, weasels,
and other modern carnivores?

78

Three early carnivores of the type called creodonts. They were
to 5 feet long. (**5-B**)

A spotted hyena from Africa. (**6–G**)

HYENA AND HYENA-TOOTH

The spotted hyena is an African beast.
It feeds on animals that get sick and die
or are killed by lions.
The hyena looks like a dog
with hind legs that are too short
to match his forelegs.
His head is bigger than a dog's head,
and his jaws are so strong
that he can crush bones easily.

Though hyenas lived in ancient Europe,
they did not come to America.
But some kinds of creodonts
looked and acted so much like hyenas
that scientists have given them a name
which means "hyena-tooth."
One hyena-tooth found in the Badlands
had a skull 12 inches long.
This beast was too clumsy to kill giant pigs
or big, strong titanotheres.
He ate the meat and crushed the bones
of dead animals.

Hyena-tooth probably lived like a real hyena. (**5–C**)

The jaguar is a big spotted cat from South America. (**6–G**)

THE CAT FAMILY

This spotted jaguar (JAG wahr) is an animal
which we often see in zoos.
It belongs to the cat family, which also
contains lions, tigers, and house cats.
No one knows how the cat family began,
but it probably came from creodonts.

82

At least 30 million years ago,
wildcats of several kinds
hunted three-toed horses and small camels.

Here are two of these ancient wildcats.
One is standing in a tree,
but the other is crouching on the ground.
Perhaps it is getting ready to pounce
upon a three-toed horse.

Two ancient cats. Their fossils are found in the Badlands. (**5–C**)

SABER-TOOTH CATS

The wildcat crouching on page 83
had long, dagger-shaped teeth
that fit against guards on the lower jaw.
This shows that the beast was a saber-tooth,
not an ancient leopard, jaguar, or tiger.
The first saber-tooth cats were not big,
though their tails were long.
As ages went by, saber-tooths grew larger
but their tails became short.
The last saber-tooths were powerful beasts.
They had big mouths that opened widely
so the teeth could be used for stabbing.
The big cats often stabbed ground sloths,
but they also ate dead animals.
Many saber-tooths once fed on mammoths
that were caught in pools of sticky tar.
In those days the pools were on a grassy plain,
but now they are part of Hancock Park,
in the city of Los Angeles.

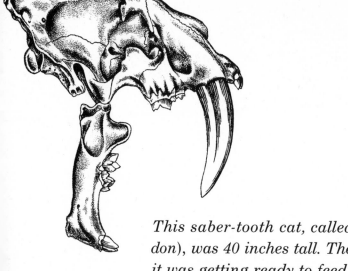

This saber-tooth cat, called Smilodon (SMY lo don), was 40 inches tall. The animal is shown as it was getting ready to feed on a mammoth that was caught in a tarpit in what is now Los Angeles. The skull shows how widely this saber-tooth could open its jaws. (6–F)

This prehistoric lion once ranged across North America. **(6–F)**

THE LARGEST LIONS

Zoo lions are big cats that come from Africa.
Male lions are larger than their mates
and have hairy manes.
A big male is 4 feet tall at the shoulder
and is 11 feet long from nose to tail.
But in prehistoric times there were lions
that stood almost 5 feet high
and were more than 13 feet long.

These beasts ranged from Mexico to Alaska,
and from California to Mississippi.
The giant lions fed on wild horses and zebras,
but they also killed camels and bison
that came to drink at pools.
Other big lions lived in Europe.
Stone-age warriors sometimes killed them
or built fires to keep the animals
out of caves in which people slept.

The big prehistoric lion (black) compared with a modern lion from Africa.

The grizzly is a big bear that now lives in the West. (**6–G**)

BEARS—LARGE AND SMALL

Bears are four-legged animals
that are carnivores, or meat-eaters.
But bears can stand up straight, like men,
and they often eat grass and berries,
or sweet foods such as honey and candy.
Grizzlies are the largest bears
that live among mountains in the West.
Many grizzlies are 3 feet 6 inches high

88

when they walk on all four feet,
and are much taller when they stand upright.
A bear that once lived in the West
was 9 inches taller than the grizzly
and about 18 inches longer.
This animal had a big, broad head,
but its face and snout were short.
The closest living relative of this giant
is the small "spectacled" bear
that is found among the mountains
of South America.

The giant bear (black) compared with a grizzly.

PRAIRIE DOGS

In some zoos you may see prairie dogs,
which once were common in the West.
Prairie dogs are not dogs at all.
They are gnawing animals, or rodents,
and are related to woodchucks and gophers.
Prairie dogs dig holes, or burrows,
that go down into the ground
for 10, 12, or even 15 feet.
The animals hide in their burrows
when they are frightened
and sleep there on cold, rainy days.
On sunny days, prairie dogs go out
to find roots, green plants, and seeds to eat.
The animals also sun themselves
beside the doors of their burrows.
There they can hide instantly
if a hawk or a man comes near.

rairie dogs are burrowing animals related to gophers and wood-ucks. They live in zoos and in the West. (**6–G**)

An ancient gopher with horns. (**5–E**)

ANCIENT BURROWERS

Prairie dogs have no horns,
but this rodent of ancient Nebraska had two.
There also were long claws on his forefeet,
which he used to dig his hole.
Another prehistoric burrower
was a small land-dwelling beaver
that also lived in Nebraska.
Land beavers dug burrows that twisted
round and round like huge corkscrews.
In time, the holes were filled with mud
that hardened into stone.

The twisted fillings are found in cliffs.
Ranchmen who find the fillings
often call them "devil's corkscrews."

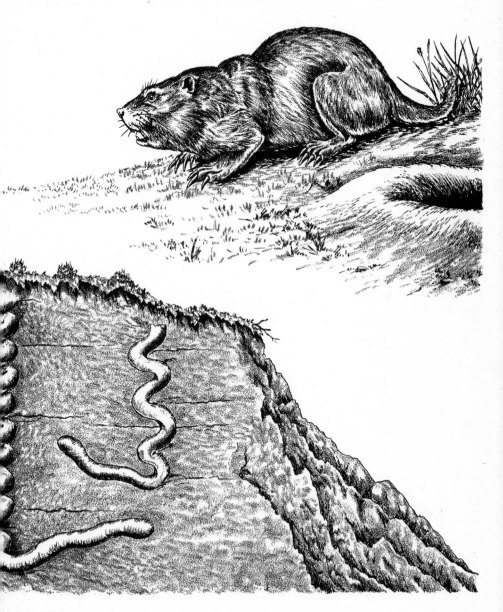

*e land beaver and two of its filled-up burrows, which are often
'led "devil's corkscrews." (**5–D**)*

A BIRD WITH TEETH

Did you ever hear a person say
that something is "scarce as hens' teeth"?
This means that the thing does not exist,
for hens and other living birds are toothless.
But our prehistoric zoo contains a bird
that had teeth and scales on its jaws.
We call it Archaeopteryx (AR kee OP ter ix),
which means "ancient bird."
Archaeopteryx lived in Europe
more than 130 million years ago.
The bird had short wings and a long tail.
Three toes showed plainly on each wing.
The tail was long, like a lizard's tail,
though feathers grew along each side.
The teeth, which were small, showed plainly
when the bird opened its mouth.
They show still more plainly when we look
at the bare, fossilized skull.

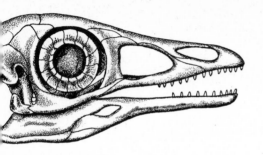

This skull of the oldest known bird, more than life size, shows its teeth and the ring of bone in the eyes. (**3**)

rchaeopteryx had teeth, a long tail, and toes on its wings. (**3**)

Two western divers on land and one in the water. (**4**)

WESTERN DIVERS

In zoos we often see penguins.
They are black-and-white birds that dive
and then swim under water with their wings,
which are shaped like oars.
In ancient times, big diving birds
lived in a sea that covered the West.
Western divers had such small wings
that they could not be seen.
The birds swam with big, paddle-shaped feet
and caught fish with their beaks.
The beaks were long and sharp,
and contained many teeth.
Western divers spent most
of their lives in the water,
for they could not fly
and their legs were not
made for walking on land.

A penguin swimming under water. (**6–G**

GIANT MOAS

Ostriches are the largest birds
to be seen in a modern zoo.
A full-grown ostrich is 8 feet tall
and weighs almost 300 pounds.
But moas, which once lived in New Zealand,
became bigger than any ostrich.
The moa called Pachyornis (PAK i OR nis),
which means "thick bird,"
had massive legs and a big body,
but was only 6 or 7 feet tall.
Dinornis (dy NOR nis), the "terrible bird,"
was 12 feet tall when he raised his head,
and weighed at least 500 pounds.
Both these moas were stupid and clumsy.
They lived in valleys and in swamps,
where they often sank into the mud.
Scientists now dig their skeletons
from the swampy ground
and take them to museums.

Two moas of prehistoric New Zealand. (**6–F**)

Eggs of a hen (1), ostrich (2), Moa (3), and Aepyornis (4).

BIG EGGS AND BIG BIRDS

An ostrich egg seems very large,
for it is 6 inches long and holds
as much as twenty-five hens' eggs.
But people on an island near southern Africa
used to find eggshells 13 inches long.
The people sawed these shells in half
to make bowls for cooking.
Scientists thought birds that laid
such eggs must have been enormous,
and named them Aepyornis (EE pi OR nis),
which means "very tall bird."

Really, Aepyornis was only 7 or 8 feet tall,
but its body and legs were very thick.
Aepyornis weighed almost a thousand pounds.
It was the biggest bird that ever lived,
even though it was 4 feet
shorter than the tallest moa.

Aepyornis was a huge bird that laid its eggs on the ground. **(6–F)**

The alligator is often seen in reptile houses of zoos. (**6–G**)

REPTILES

The reptile house in a zoo
is a warm building that contains
lizards, snakes, tortoises, turtles,
and sleepy alligators.
The reptile house is heated because
these creatures cannot warm themselves,
as birds and hairy animals do.
Reptiles have scales, not hair or feathers,
but turtles also have thick shells,
and so do land-dwelling tortoises.

102

Reptiles came into existence long before
there were birds or hairy animals
such as horses, cats, and creodonts.
Snakes are reptiles that lost their legs,
and some ancient lizards looked like fish.
Other reptiles have hardly changed
for millions and millions of years.
Modern alligators resemble those
that lived when titanotheres were common.
This tortoise is even older.
Still, you can hardly tell it
from big, clumsy tortoises
that are kept in many modern zoos.

This ancient tortoise looked like some big modern kinds. (**5–B**)

FALSE ALLIGATOR

If you had lived 170 million years ago,
you might have seen this false alligator
sunning himself in a swamp.
The man who first found a reptile like this
called it a phytosaur (FY toe sawr)
because he thought it fed on plants.
We now know that the creature
looked and acted like an alligator
and ate fish or other reptiles.
We can tell this by the long, sharp teeth,
but we know that phytosaurs
were false (not real) alligators
when we look at their nostrils.
An alligator's nostrils are on its snout,
and so are the nostrils of a crocodile.
But a phytosaur's nostrils were near its eyes.
The reptile could breathe easily
while its body and even its snout
were lying under water.

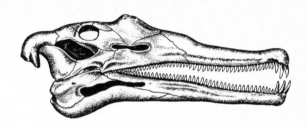

...lse alligators, or phytosaurs, were found in many parts of the ...rld. This big one, about 20 feet long, lived in what is now the ...trified Forest, in northeastern Arizona. The reptile's skull is ...own above. (**2**)

FINBACK FROM TEXAS

Strange lizards of several kinds
are kept in the reptile houses of zoos.
But no modern lizard is as strange
as Finback, which lived in Texas
more than 200 million years ago.
Finback, or Dimetrodon (dy MET roe don),
had a long tail and a big head,
with sharp, dagger-shaped teeth.
Bony spines grew from the reptile's back.
Skin spread between the spines,
forming a broad "sail" or "fin"
that was 2 to 4 feet high.
Finback killed other reptiles,
and bit off pieces of meat.

No one knows what the "fin" was good for.
It could not be used in swimming,
for Finback lived on land.
He probably did not even wade
in shallow rivers or in ponds.

inback had a big head, a long tail, and a "fin" or "sail" on his ack. (**1**)

A GIANT DINOSAUR

Dinosaurs were the strangest reptiles
in the prehistoric zoo,
and some of them were the largest.
At the front of the book you will see
a very strange dinosaur (DY no sawr)
with a bony crest on his head.
Here is one of the biggest dinosaurs,
known as Brachiosaurus (BRAK i o SAW rus).
Brachiosaurus was 75 feet long,
and his head was 40 feet above the ground.
This huge reptile weighed about 40 tons,
or as much as ten elephants.
Brachiosaurus lived in swamps,
where he waded and ate juicy plants.
Other dinosaur giants were waders, too.
Some kinds were longer than Brachiosaurus,
but their bodies were not so big.
This meant that they were not so heavy,
though they weighed 20 to 30 tons.

rachiosaurus, the largest dinosaur, lived in swamps and ate icy plants. He weighed about 40 tons. (**3**)

MEAT-EATING HUNTERS

The biggest dinosaurs ate plants,
which were plentiful in swamps.
Many smaller dinosaurs became meat-eaters
that hunted other reptiles.
The meat-eaters had big heads and mouths
with many dagger-shaped teeth.
These reptiles walked on their hind legs
with their tails held out to balance their bodies.
Here are two meat-eating dinosaurs
that prowled in forests near the swamps
and even waded through shallow water
as they followed the big plant-eaters.
Although these meat-eaters were not giants,
Allosaurus (AL lo SAW rus) was 34 feet long
and 14 feet tall when he raised his head.
Ceratosaurus (SEHR a toe SAW rus)
was much smaller.
Still, he was many times larger
than any meat-eating reptile
that lives on land today.

Ceratosaurus

Allosaurus

Two meat-eating dinosaurs. (**3**)

STUPID STEGOSAURUS

We sometimes call this the plated dinosaur
because two rows of bony plates
were fastened to the creature's back.
A better name is Stegosaurus (STEG o SAW rus),
for it is the one scientists use.
Stegosaurus was a peaceful plant-eater
that had a tiny, stupid brain.
He lived in woods where Allosaurus hunted,
but he could not run away from danger,
and he could not escape from meat-eaters
by wading into deep water.
Instead, he stood still and swung his tail,
which was armed with bony spines
that could crush the ribs of Allosaurus.
Stegosaurus controlled his tail with a ganglion,
or "extra brain," above his hips.
This "extra brain" was much larger
than the real brain
in this stupid dinosaur's head.

Real brain

*"Second brain,"
or ganglion*

The stupid, plate-backed Stegosaurus. (**3**)

Triceratops, a beaked dinosaur with horns. (**4**)

DINOSAURS WITH BEAKS

We call many reptiles dinosaurs,
as if they were closely related.
Really, these creatures belonged
to two quite different groups.
The dinosaurs in one group were beakless
and only a few kinds had horns.
The other group of dinosaurs had beaks
and several kinds possessed horns.
Stegosaurus was a beaked dinosaur.

114

So was Triceratops (try SAIR a TOPS),
which had three horns and a hooked beak,
as well as a bony shield for his neck.
Triceratops lived on dry land,
but duckbills often waded or swam
with their webbed feet and broad tails.
Some duckbills had low, flat heads,
but the one at the front of this book
had a bony crest that divided
like the antlers of some deer.

A duck-billed dinosaur. (**4**)

THE TYRANT REPTILE

The hunting dinosaurs on page 111
lived when Brachiosaurus and other giants
were found in many parts of the world.
As time passed, the giants died out,
but some hunting dinosaurs kept on living.
By the time Triceratops roamed in the West,
new kinds of meat-eaters had become
much larger than Allosaurus.
The largest meat-eater is named
Tyrannosaurus (ty RAN o SAW rus),
which means "tyrant reptile."
The tyrant was 47 feet long and 18 feet tall,
and his mouth was almost 3 feet wide.
He ate any reptile he could kill.
Perhaps he often attacked Triceratops,
who protected himself with his shield
and with his long, sharp horns.

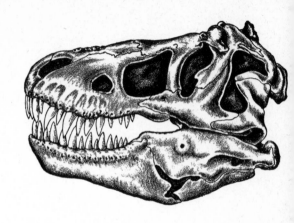

Skull of the tyrant reptile, almost 4 feet long.

Tyrannosaurus, the tyrant reptile, was 18 feet tall. (**4**)

These small dinosaurs were about 6 feet long. (**2**)

HOW BIG WAS HUGE?

We have described some huge dinosaurs,
telling how large they were.
Another way to show how big dinosaurs were
is to draw a man between two leg bones
of Brachiosaurus and another giant
which is often called the "thunder lizard."
Both bones are taller than the man,
and the whole reptiles
were many times larger still.

118

Even "small" dinosaurs were bigger
than most modern reptiles.
The "small" dinosaur on page 118
was 6 feet long and weighed 50 pounds.
It was twice as long
and at least four times as heavy
as most of the large lizards
kept in the reptile houses of zoos.

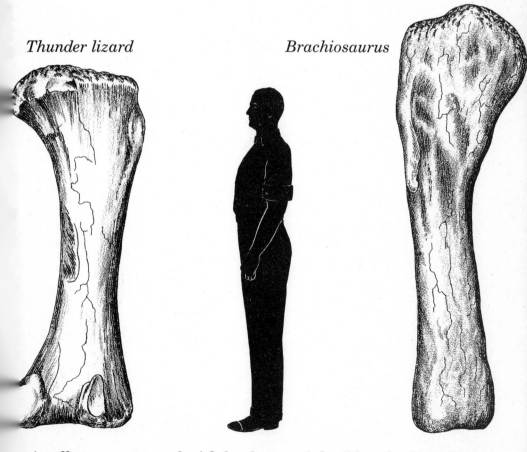

Thunder lizard   *Brachiosaurus*

A tall man compared with leg bones of the "thunder lizard" and Brachiosaurus.

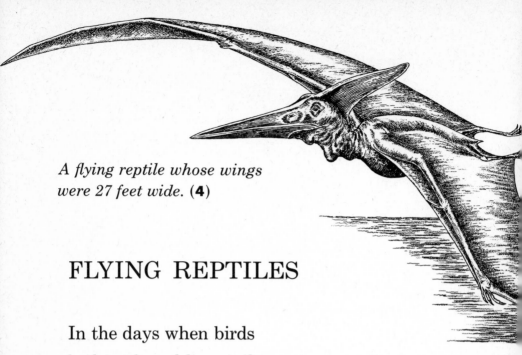

*A flying reptile whose wings
were 27 feet wide.* (**4**)

FLYING REPTILES

In the days when birds
had teeth and long tails,
some reptiles developed wings
that were covered with skin.
At first these flying reptiles were small,
and some kinds became still smaller.
But as time went by, others grew so large
that their wings were 20 to 27 feet wide.
These broad-winged creatures lost their teeth
and developed birdlike beaks.
They also had bony crests on their heads.
Crests helped the reptiles balance themselves
when they flew over shallow seas
or swooped down to catch the fish
which were their favorite food.

120

Two small flying reptiles with teeth, not beaks. (**3**)

MOSASAUR, OR SEA-LIZARD

This reptile, called a mosasaur (MO sa sawr),
was closely related to lizards
although it lived in the sea.
Its body had become long and fishlike
and its legs had turned into flippers,
which looked almost like fins.
The first mosasaurs were not large,
but in time they became powerful creatures
which were 20 to 50 feet long.
Here is a mosasaur that lived in a sea
that covered Kansas and other regions
more than 60 million years ago.
The reptile ate fish and turtles,
as well as other sea-dwelling creatures.
Perhaps the big, hungry sea-lizard
also caught western divers
or snapped at flying reptiles
when they swooped close to the water
while they were looking for fish.

122

Bones in the left front flipper of a mosasaur.

Mosasaurs were lizards that swam in the sea. (**4**)

CALENDAR OF ANCIENT AGES

In order to tell when something happened
we look at a calendar that divides time
into months, weeks, and days.
Scientists who find out what happened
during ancient, or prehistoric, times
have a longer calendar.
It divides the earth's history
into eras, ages, and epochs
and tells when they began.
Here is part of this long calendar.
It lists all the eras, ages, and epochs
during which the animals described in this book
lived upon our earth.
When you use the calendar, remember this fact:

The earliest era and age are at the bottom.
The youngest, or most recent, age and era
are shown at the top.

124

CALENDAR OF ANCIENT AGES

Eras	Ages and Epochs	When they began	Some typical animals

CENOZOIC (Era of Mammals)	**(6)** Quaternary Age
	  (G) Recent Epoch
	  (F) Ice "Age," or Epoch
		Less than one million years ago	In recent times, many large animals died out. Mammoths, mastodons, big bison, and the last of the saber-tooths. Big birds in Africa and New Zealand.

	(5) Tertiary Age
	  (E) Pliocene Epoch
	  (D) Miocene Epoch
	  (C) Oligocene Epoch
	  (B) Eocene Epoch
	  (A) Paleocene Epoch
		12 million
		28 million
		40 million
		50 million
		60 million
		years ago
			Animals with warm blood and hair, which we call mammals. At first they were very different from modern mammals. But as epochs passed, new ones developed, becoming more and more like creatures that live today.

MESOZOIC (Era of Reptiles)	**(4)** Cretaceous Age	130 million years ago	Dinosaurs with beaks and crests or horns; big meat-eaters such as the tyrant reptile. Flying reptiles, mosasaurs, western divers.
	(3) Jurassic Age	155 million years ago	Big plant-eating dinosaurs and smaller meat-eaters. Early flying reptiles and birds with teeth.
	(2) Triassic Age	185 million years ago	False alligators and the first dinosaurs. Most of them were small, but some other reptiles became big.
PALEOZOIC (Ancient Era)	**(1)** Permian Age	210 million years ago	Finback and other early reptiles. Also creatures that resembled salamanders.
	Several early ages and epochs, and still more ancient eras.	Most of the animals that lived in these very ancient times were sea-dwellers that had no backbones. Since their relatives are not in zoos, they are not described in this book.	

INDEX

126

127

A dinosaur with horns and a beak. (**4**)